DR. OBOT TIGAH

LIVE BY
HIGH
STANDARDS

A 40-DAY
DEVOTIONAL
TO RENEW
YOUR MIND

& LIVE THE LIFE
GOD INTENDED

For speaking engagements, please contact:
Dr. Obot Tigah via email – obot@girlswithstandards.com

Connect with Dr. Obot Tigah on all social media platforms: https://linktr.ee/Obot.Tigah

Join the Girls With Standards community by signing up on our website https://girlswithstandards.com/ or by connecting with us on YouTube www.youtube.com/girlswithstandards, Instagram www.instagram.com/girls_withstandards, TikTok https://www.tiktok.com/@girlswithstandards, and Facebook.

CONTENTS

INTRODUCTION

In November 2018, God-inspired me to start a ministry that would equip young women with tools, resources, and strategies to live according to the standards of His word. This idea evolved into Girls With Standards ministry as we know it today. Before the inception of the ministry, and before I understood my worth in Christ, I also lived below God's standards for my life. I was surrounded by girls and women who did not know their true worth and value either. However, everything changed when I became a Christian. I gradually came to realize my worth in Christ. Now, I am on a mission to help other women know their worth in Christ and to live up to the high standards that He has graciously and lovingly provided in His word.

The first step to knowing your worth in Christ is to spend time reading what God says about you in His word. This is the foundation for living a life of purpose and fulfilment. This devotional was written to help you develop the daily habit of spending time in the word and in prayer. I believe that as you spend time daily in the word and prayer, you will no longer be conformed to the low standards of this world, but will live according to the high standards God has provided for you in His word.

How to Use this Devotional

Pick a place and time to read this devotional. Ideally, in the morning, before your day begins, and in a quiet place. Make sure you have a pen and the Live by High Standards Devotional Journal (or any notebook) as you read. Each devotional begins with a "focus scripture" and "daily scripture reading". Before you begin, say these words of prayer: Dear Heavenly Father, I thank You for the opportunity to read Your word today. Open my eyes to see what You want me to see. Open my ears to hear what You want me to hear. Soften my heart to receive the instruction, correction, direction, and encouragement that I need today. May Your word not be mere words on paper; may they be spirit and life to me. In Jesus' name I have prayed. Amen.

After you have prayed, begin your devotion by reading the daily scripture reading, and write down any thoughts that come to your mind as you read. Don't worry about the content; just write down your thoughts. It could be anything, ranging from what stood out to you from the passage, what you think God wants you to do, how you will implement what you have learned and read, and so on. You can also write down the questions you may have about the passage or what you found surprising while reading.

After that, read the devotional, and take note of the parts that stood out to you. At the end of each devotional, answer the questions in the Reflection section in your journal or any notebook. Then say the recommended prayers along with any other prayers you feel led to say. Next, review the Practical Applications, and plan to implement them that day and in the days to come. After this, read the Focus Scripture again, memorize it, and think about the words throughout the day. This is known as meditation.

I have prayed for you, and I believe that you will experience true transformation and growth as you spend time daily in the word and in prayer. I love you. Most importantly, the Maker of heaven and earth, the One who made you in His image, loves you fiercely and is rooting for you.

1

Do You Have High Standards?

Focus Scripture

Do not conform yourselves to the standards of this world, but let God transform you inwardly by a complete change of your mind. Then you will be able to know the will of God--what is good and is pleasing to him and is perfect.

Romans 12:2 (GNB)

Daily Scripture Reading: Romans 12

The Oxford English Dictionary, defines the word, standard as a level of quality or attainment. It also defines it as an idea or thing used as a measure, norm, or model in comparative evaluations. Simply put, a standard is a principle that you live by. Meaning, girls with standards will not do certain things because everyone is doing it.

I know that having standards have been perceived as a bad thing. In fact, I've heard people advise women and even men to "lower their standards" if they want to achieve x, y, or z. Regardless of what people say, do not lower your standards. Have high standards and live by them. Don't settle for anything or anyone in the name of lowering your expectations. Just so we're on the same page, the standards I am referring to are not a list of rules that I made up. They are the ones found in God's word.

In whatever you think, say, or do, live according to the standards of God's word. Our key scripture in Romans 12:2 admonishes us not to conform to the standards of this world but to be transformed inwardly by renewing our minds through God's word. We renew our minds by changing our thoughts to reflect what God says in His word. As a man thinks in his heart, so is he (Proverbs 23:7). So the first step to living by the standards of God is to let His word change your mind.

This change cannot happen if you do not know what the word says. And believe me, there is nothing you will encounter in life that God has not already addressed in His word. But you have to know what the word says to apply it to your life.

I want to challenge you to commit to reading at least one chapter of the Bible per day this year. The Bible can be overwhelming sometimes, but using a daily devotional like this one or the Bible app can help guide you on where to read. There are different reading plans on the Bible app to help get you started. Make a decision to read the Bible daily today!

Reflect
How can you make time to read the Bible more this year? What activities or tasks can you give up to make room for daily Bible reading?

Pray
Dear Lord, I have learned that I must live by the standards of Your word and not by the standards of this world. Please, help me to read the Bible daily so that I can renew my mind and live according to Your standards. In Jesus' name I pray. Amen.

Practical Application
1. Set a time daily for Bible study.
2. Make Bible reading the first thing you do when you wake up.
3. Share your commitment to reading the Bible daily with a like-minded friend who can keep you accountable. Send a text to that friend after you have completed your daily reading and encourage them to do the same.

2

GOD IS TRUE TO HIS WORD

Focus Scripture

So shall My word be that goes forth from My mouth; It shall not return to Me void, But it shall accomplish what I please, And it shall prosper in the thing for which I sent it.

Isaiah 55:11 (NKJV)

Daily Scripture Reading: Genesis 15-16

When God speaks, His word surely comes to pass. Therefore, we owe it to ourselves and our descendants to hold on to His word and not let the enemy make us impatient while we wait for the fulfillment of His word in our lives. Our patience comes with a blessing, just as our impatience comes with consequences.

In today's scripture reading in Genesis 15, God made a covenant with Abraham (previously Abram). God promised to give him a son and make him the father of many nations. He believed in God, and it was accounted to him for righteousness. However, somewhere in between when God made the promise to him and the fulfillment, he stopped believing.

His disbelief was made evident in his actions in the next chapter (Genesis 16). Sarah, his wife, had also stopped believing in God's promise to give her a son. Instead of waiting patiently for the word to be fulfilled in her life and that of her husband, she decided to "help" God accomplish it. She offered her maid, Hagar, to Abraham so they could have a son. Her action was an error with consequences that still affect us today.

It is important to know that God's blessings make us rich and add no sorrow to it. On the contrary, trying to "help" God accomplish what He spoke over our lives will bring sorrow, pain, and regret. Our impatience will prevent us from not fully enjoying the blessing God intended for us because there will be an "Ishmael" in the mix.

I want to encourage you to hold on to the promises of God for your life. His word never fails! The enemy and circumstances may tempt you to be impatient, but hold on to the promise. Remind yourself daily what the word says about any situation you are facing and hold on to it.

Reflect
What promises from God are you still waiting for? What can you do to wait patiently for the fulfillment of that promise(s)?

Pray
Dear Lord, I have learned today that You keep Your word. You are faithful, and whatever You say comes to pass at the appointed time. Please help me to trust and obey You. Give me the grace to patiently wait for You to fulfill Your promises to me. In Jesus' name I pray. Amen.

Practical Applications
1. Write down God's promises for your life.
2. Review the list often and check-off those that have been fulfilled.
3. Regularly remind yourself of the promises that are yet to be fulfilled and pray about them.

3

— • —

WALKING WITH GOD IN AN EVIL WORLD

Focus Scripture

This is the account of Noah and his family. Noah was a righteous man, the only blameless person living on earth at the time, and he walked in close fellowship with God.

Genesis 6:9 (NLT)

Daily Scripture Reading: Genesis 6-7

In a world where everyone is doing what they want, it is still possible to walk in close fellowship with God. Our scripture reading in Genesis chapter 6 tells the story of Noah and how he was the only just person in his generation. Let that sink in. To be the only righteous person at that time must have been really difficult and an accomplishment that required a lot of discipline.

Fortunately, we are not alone in our quest for righteousness in today's world. Many other believers are striving to daily walk in close fellowship with God in a world where the temptation to do the opposite is enormous. And, while some of us are surrounded by fellow believers, some people live in cities and countries where they are the only ones making an effort to walk with God. Even in those cases, it is still possible to walk with God. For with God nothing will be impossible (Luke 1:37 NKJV).

Walking with God has multiple benefits. Just as God protected Noah from the destruction that came upon the world, He will protect us. When we walk with God, He shares His secret plans with us, just like He did with Noah. A gesture that saved him and his family from perishing.

God gave Noah instructions on how to build the ark to survive the flood. In the same way, He has given us instructions through His word on how to be preserved in this evil world. Our protection and preservation come from obeying His word. Make a decision to walk with Him today, regardless of what other people around you are doing.

Reflect
Do you have people around you who are striving to walk with God in this evil world? What can you do to encourage yourself or other believers to keep walking with God?

Pray
Dear Lord, I have learned today that it is possible to live a holy and righteous life in this world. You have given us everything we need for life and godliness in Your word. Give us the strength not to be moved by the wickedness around us but to continue to walk with You. Connect us with people who may be struggling to walk with You due to circumstances beyond their control and give us the wisdom to encourage them. In Jesus' name I pray. Amen.

Practical Applications
1. Make a list of people around you whom you can go to when in need of spiritual encouragement. Surround yourself with such people and reach out when you are struggling.
2. Make a list of people who may be struggling in their walk with God and pray for them.
3. Pray daily for the grace and strength to remain without spot in this world.

4

PRIORITIES

Focus Scripture

*But seek first the kingdom of God and His righteousness, and all
these things shall be added unto you.*

Matthew 6:33 (NKJV)

Daily Scripture Reading: Matthew 6

We live in a world where worrying about food, clothing, and shelter is almost
inevitable. We hear about people who are homeless, famished, and/or unable
to provide for their daily needs. This may cause us to wonder if we will have
similar unpleasant experiences. God has called us to trust Him and His ability
to provide for all our needs despite the realities of life.

The Lord invites us to consider the birds of the air, the lilies and grass of the
field, and how he takes care of them. The birds of the air do not worry about
food, neither do the lilies and grass of the field worry about clothing, yet they are
fed sumptuous meals and clothed beautifully daily! How much more will our
Heavenly Father feed, clothe, and provide shelter for us His precious children?

Jesus admonishes that the solution for worrying about the basic needs of life is to
seek the kingdom of God and His righteousness first, and all these things (food,
clothing, and shelter) will be added unto us. But what exactly is the kingdom
of God? We cannot seek the kingdom of God first if we do not know what

it is. The kingdom of God is righteousness, peace, and joy in the Holy Spirit (Romans 14:17, NKJV). The kingdom of God is God's will done on earth as it is in heaven. In the Lord's prayer, Jesus encouraged His disciples to pray for the kingdom of God before their daily bread (Matthew 6:10-11). This is because all our needs are met in God's kingdom, so when we pray for God's kingdom to come, we are inevitably praying for our needs to be met.

Reflect
How have you prioritized seeking the kingdom of God first in your daily life? If your priorities are misplaced, what steps can you take to seek God's kingdom first?

Pray
Dear Heavenly Father, I thank You because You made me and You care deeply for me. You know that I have needs, and You have made provisions to meet them all if I seek Your kingdom first. I know that I have not been diligent in seeking You first before anything else. I repent and ask You to give me the grace to seek Your kingdom first by spending time with You daily. In Jesus' name I pray. Amen.

Practical Applications
1. Make spending time with God your number one priority each day.
2. Make a commitment not to speak with anyone until you have spoken to God first.
3. Thank God daily that all your needs are met as you seek Him first.

5

— • —

FEAR AND OBEDIENCE

Focus Scripture

The fear of the Lord is the beginning of wisdom, and the knowledge of the Holy One is understanding.

Proverbs 9:10 (NKJV)

Daily Scripture Reading: Proverbs 9

Fear means to be afraid or be in awe of something or someone with great power. People often obey powerful individuals out of fear because they know that disobedience can lead to dire consequences, even death. It is no news that God is powerful; He is the creator of the heavens and the earth. He made all the things we see on Earth. The earth and everything that is in it belong to Him. The earth is also His footstool. Think about the most powerful human you know. Whoever you come up with does not remotely come close to being as powerful as God.

When you know that someone has the power to do whatever they want with your life, it forces obedience. Rulers, kings, and leaders are examples of powerful people. However, God is omnipotent, all-powerful! The Hebrew midwives in Egypt recognized this fact when they chose to obey God rather than Pharaoh, the king of Egypt. Pharaoh had instructed them to kill the sons of the Hebrew women, but the midwives feared God and did not do what the king commanded them to do. They were afraid of two powerful entities: the king of Egypt and the King of kings. However, they understood that God was more powerful than the Egyptian king, and it was better to obey God.

In our daily lives, we will experience situations where we will need to choose whom to obey. Do I obey my boss, my friend, or the president? Jesus gives us a clear path in Matthew 10:28 when he instructs us to fear the One [God] who can destroy both the soul and the body, rather than the one who is only able to destroy the body. I encourage you to choose to obey God.

Fearing and obeying Him has so many earthly and eternal rewards. The midwives multiplied, grew mighty, and enjoyed favor and provision because they feared God and obeyed Him. Even if obeying God can lead to bad earthly outcomes, like losing favor with a powerful person or even death, still choose obedience to God. While obeying the Lord may have earthly rewards, the eternal rewards are far greater and should be your aim.

Reflect
What consequences are you afraid of when you choose to obey a powerful person rather than God? Are the earthly consequences of disobeying a powerful person worth your soul?

Pray
Omnipotent God, forgive me for the times I obeyed other people instead of You. Help me to be courageous and to obey You even when the consequences are scary. Help me to be like the Hebrew midwives who feared God and did not do as the king of Egypt commanded them. Instill in me a deep fear of You and Your commandments. In Jesus' name I pray. Amen.

Practical Applications
1. When you need to make decisions, determine if your choice will lead to obedience to God or obedience to man.
2. Decide to obey God regardless of the circumstances and/or the consequences.
3. Pray for grace, strength, and courage to obey God in all situations.

6

— ◦ —

THE WEALTH COVENANT

Focus Scripture

And you shall remember the Lord your God, for it is He who gives you power to get wealth, that He may establish His covenant which He swore to your fathers, as it is this day.

Deuteronomy 8:18

Daily Scripture Reading: Deuteronomy 8

A covenant is a binding agreement between two people, and it is often sealed with blood. The Bible gives numerous accounts of covenants God made with His people: the Noahic covenant (Genesis 9:8-17), the Abrahamic covenant (Genesis 12 and 15), the Mosaic covenant (Exodus 19:1-6; 24:1-8), the Davidic covenant (2 Samuel 7:1-17), and the New covenant (Jeremiah 21:31-34; Luke 22:14-20). God takes covenants seriously, and He remembers them forever (Psalm 105:8).

The Abrahamic covenant is also known as the wealth covenant. It is the covenant God made with Abraham in Genesis 12 and 15 to bless him and his descendants abundantly, so that they would, in turn, become a blessing to others. As descendants of Abraham, this covenant is automatically at work in our lives. However, we need power (vigor, strength, force, capacity, means, or substance) to get wealth. And this power comes from the Lord.

God is committed to keeping His covenant of wealth with all Abraham's descendants. Consequently, God will give us the power to get wealth if we ask Him. The power to get wealth can come from God-given gifts/talents, ideas, strategies, relationships, or mentorships. It can also come from physical strength, tenacity, and obedience to God's word.

With the blessings of wealth comes responsibility. When the Lord has blessed you and given you power, do not forget Him. Remember that we are stewards of the resources God entrusts to us. Thus, the Lord expects us to use our wealth to serve His purposes, to be a blessing to others, and to recognize that all we have comes from Him.

Reflect
What power do you need to get wealth? How can you receive power to get wealth? When God blesses you with wealth, how will you serve His purposes? How will you be a blessing to others? What will you do to ensure that you do not forget the Source of your wealth?

Pray
God of covenants, thank You because I am a descendant of Abraham and a partaker of the Abrahamic covenant. Lord, Your word says You give us power to get wealth, and I understand that it can come in different forms. Lord, help me to identify and use the power I already have to tap into this abundance. If there is something I am lacking that can help me get wealth, provide it. Open my eyes to see the resources You have already placed around me. Help me to be diligent in using the power You have given me to get wealth. And when I become wealthy, may I not forget You, the source. Help me use my wealth to advance Your kingdom and to be a blessing to others. In Jesus' name I pray. Amen.

Practical Applications
1. Write down your gifts, talents, and resources.
2. Explore ways you can convert your gifts, talents, and ideas into a source or sources of income.
3. Take a step of faith and launch those ideas.

7

LIP SERVICE OR HEART SERVICE?

Focus Scripture

He answered and said to them, "Well did Isaiah prophesy of you hypocrites, as it is written: These people honor Me with their lips, but their heart is far from Me.

Mark 7:6

Daily Scripture Reading: Mark 7

Lip service means expressing allegiance to someone or something in words without backing it up with actions. Heart service means your actions align with what is in your heart. If we are true to ourselves, whatever is in our hearts, good or bad, will eventually be expressed in our speech and actions. People who engage in lip service often say things that do not truly reflect what is in their hearts. The main aim of those people who pay lip service is to prevent their listeners and spectators from knowing the true state of their hearts.

The Scripture is filled with many instances where Jesus warned us against acting like the hypocrites. Hypocrites are religious people who put on an act to appear to love the Lord and obey His commandments, but whose hearts are far from what they say and do. Jesus encourages us to practice heart service, to let what is in our hearts dictate our words and actions.

This kind of service requires an intimate relationship with the Holy Spirit. Jeremiah 17:9 says that the heart is desperately wicked and deceitful, who can know it? To genuinely live out what is in our hearts, we need the help of the Holy Spirit to weed out every form of wickedness. We must be like David and ask the Lord to search our hearts to see if there is any wicked way in us, and to lead us in the everlasting way (Psalm 123:23-24).

Heart service requires us to guard our hearts with all diligence because everything we do flows from it. Since our words and actions come from our hearts, we must plant good things in our hearts. We can store up good treasures there by paying attention to what we see, read, say, who/what we listen to, where we go, and our circles of influence. We must read, obey, and meditate on the word of God daily.

Reflect
In what areas are your words and actions mismatched? How can you determine what is truly in your heart? If your heart has evil treasures, how can you replace them with good treasures?

Pray
Dear Lord, I want my words and actions to match what is in my heart. Search my heart, oh God. Try me, and know my thoughts. Psalm 139:23 says that as a man thinks in his heart, so is he. Expose the thoughts of my heart that are wicked, and lead me in the everlasting way. Holy Spirit, help me to be a true follower and lover of God. In Jesus' name I pray. Amen.

Practical Applications
1. Guard your heart with all diligence because the issues of life flow out of it (Proverbs 4:23).
2. Check the state of your heart regularly.
3. Learn to say no when your heart is not fully committed to something.

8

---◆---

TIMES AND SEASONS

Focus Scripture

To everything there is a season, a time for every purpose under heaven.

Ecclesiastes 3:1

Daily Scripture Reading: Ecclesiastes 3

Time can be defined as an appointed period in which events occur. It moves irreversibly from the past, through the present, and into the future. Understanding that every event has its appointed time can make us use our time wisely and be sensitive to seasons.

Ecclesiastes 3:1-8 lists examples of events that must occur at specific times. Verse 11 reminds us that God has made everything beautiful in its time. This means that when things occur outside their appointed times, the beauty intended for that event may not be actualized. One example is the process of conception, pregnancy, and childbirth. For a woman to become pregnant, the male sperm must be readily available at the time the ovum is released. Fertilization, which is the meeting of the ovum and sperm, must occur within a specific time frame to result in pregnancy. Also, the woman must remain pregnant for a period of 37-42 weeks before the baby is born. A birth that occurs before or after this time frame can lead to undesirable complications for both the mother and her unborn baby.

The Lord expects us to be discerning of the different times and seasons of our lives (Luke 12:54-56). The first step to knowing what to do per season is knowing times and seasons we are in (1 Chronicles 12:32). Once you have discovered the season you are in, do what is expected of you. If you are in a season of planting, plant. When it is time to harvest what has been planted, do so. Do not let the circumstances around you determine what you should do in each season; let the season dictate what you should do (Ecclesiastes 11:4). Strive to apply this principle to every facet of your life. This might be challenging sometimes, but with God, all things are possible (Matthew 19:26).

Reflect
How do you determine the season of life that you are in? What can you do to achieve the purpose of this season?

Pray
Dear Lord, give me an understanding of the various times and seasons of my life, and help me to do what is required of me in each season. May I not let circumstances prevent me from doing what I need to do in each season. Help me overcome the challenges associated with each season. I pray that I will experience beauty in every phase of my life. In Jesus' name I pray. Amen.

Practical Applications
1. Pray for the spirit of discernment to identify the various seasons of your life.
2. Pray and ask God what you need to do in each season.
3. Do what needs to be done in every season of life, regardless of the circumstances.

9

STEWARDSHIP

Focus Scripture

Moreover, it is required in stewards that one be found faithful.

1 Corinthians 4:2

Daily Scripture Reading: Luke 16

A steward is someone who has been given the responsibility to care for another person's property. In Psalm 24:1, God says that everything in the world belongs to Him, from people to property, and animals. Everything you can think of that exists on the earth belongs to God. In Genesis 1 and 2, after God had created Adam and Eve, He gave them dominion over everything He created and made them stewards of the earth and all that is in it.

An important requirement of stewards is faithfulness. Faithful stewards are committed to caring for what has been entrusted to them, even when they are not being supervised. With whatever wealth or resources we have, no matter how little, God expects us to be faithful stewards of those resources. The stewards who have been faithful with little will inevitably receive more.

Being a faithful steward of earthly resources is a prelude to being entrusted with eternal riches. All earthly riches belong to God, and when this life is over, we will not take those riches with us to heaven because they do not belong to us (1

Timothy 6:7). We are mere stewards of those resources. However, faithfulness in stewarding God's earthly riches, prepares us for receiving true riches that will last forever, riches that will belong to us for eternity (Matthew 6:20).

To please God with how we use the resources He has entrusted to us, we must seek guidance from Him. When we acknowledge that whatever we have comes from Him, He will direct us on how to use His resources. Some practical ways of stewarding God's resources include giving back to Him in tithes and offerings (Malachi 3:10), helping the poor and needy (Deuteronomy 15:11), funding God's work on earth (1 Chronicles 29:2-3), caring for our family (1 Timothy 5:8), not being wasteful (Luke 16:1-2), and multiplying what He has given us through prudent investments (Matthew 25:14-23). When you are faithful with little, God will give you more. Be a faithful steward.

Reflect
Do you recognize that everything you have comes from God? Are you a good steward of the resources God has given you? In what ways are you ensuring that you are stewarding the resources you have been given?

Pray
Dear Lord, forgive me for when I have been unfaithful with the resources You have committed to my care. Give me wisdom to know what to do with these resources. Teach me ways to multiply them for Your glory. In Jesus' name I pray. Amen.

Practical Applications
1. Care for the things you have like they belong to God because they do.
2. Thank God for the things you have and continue to trust Him for more.
3. Remember that your soul is worth more than everything in this world. Do not strive to gain the whole world and lose your soul.

10

—•—

JEALOUSY

Focus Scripture

Let us not become conceited, provoking one another, envying one another.

Galatians 5:26

Daily Scripture Reading: Genesis 4 and Galatians 5

Jealousy can be defined as a feeling of discontentment due to someone else's achievements or success. Jealousy or envy can lead to anger, sadness, murder, and sin. Sin is anything that separates us from God or His presence. The first account of jealousy in the Bible is in Genesis 4, where Cain was jealous of his brother Abel. He was jealous of his brother because God accepted Abel's offering and rejected his own.

People become jealous when they compare themselves with others. Jealousy is a work of the flesh and as followers of Jesus, we have crucified the flesh, with its passions and desires on the cross. This means that we no longer live according to our feelings or act on what we are feeling. And the only way to achieve this is to live and walk in the Spirit and not do what our flesh wants us to do (Galatians 5:16).

Walking in the Spirit can be difficult, but we do not have to do it in our own strength. The Holy Spirit is available to help us in areas where we are weak. The first step to walking in the Spirit is to be honest about how you feel and bring those feelings to Jesus in prayer. God is omniscient, and He already knows what you are feeling and thinking. As believers, the Holy Spirit lives within us to reveal and convict us of sin so that we can repent.

Reflect

What achievements of other people do you desire? Are those achievements in line with what God has for you? How can you determine what God has called you to do and focus on achieving those regardless of what other people are doing?

Pray

Dear Lord, forgive me for times when I have compared myself with others and when I have been jealous of other people's accomplishments. Help me to be content with where I am and what You have given me. Help me to continue to work towards attaining all that You have for me. I remove every seed of discontentment and jealousy from my heart and mind. In Jesus' name I pray. Amen.

Practical Applications

1. Know that God loves all His children equally and unconditionally.

2. Remember that everyone has a gift. Focus on developing your gifts and talents; do not compare yourself with others.

3. Measure your growth by how far you have come, not by how far others have gone. Selah.

11

— ✦ —

ALTARS

Focus Scripture

Then the Lord appeared to Abram and said, "To your descendants I will give this land." And there he built an altar to the Lord, who had appeared to him.

Genesis 12:7

Daily Scripture Reading: Genesis 12

After the death of Abraham's father, Terah, the Lord instructed him to leave his country, family, and father's house to an unknown land. The land was the place God had chosen to establish His covenant of blessing with Abraham. He obeyed. But, when he arrived there, the land was already occupied by the Canaanites. This could be our reality, too. We do what God tells us to do, but the promises are not fulfilled immediately. What we do while we wait for the realization of God's promise is very important. Abraham set a good example for us in Genesis 12:7. He did not lose faith in God's promise. He built an altar unto the Lord to remind himself of the promises.

An altar is a designated place of worship. It is also a memorial of the place where God had a personal encounter with us, or a memorial we establish to remind us of what God has said to us. Although altars can be physical, building one is not always feasible. However, we can raise an altar of prayer in our homes, offices, hearts, or anywhere without physical props. It can even be in the form of a journal, where we record God's promises to us during our encounters with Him.

Documenting the things He says to us and going back to review them is essential. Most times, when God gives us a word, in our secret place, there is usually a window of waiting for the tangible manifestations. This is why an altar is necessary. An altar is not for God, but for us. It reminds us of what God has said and keeps us on track. God never forgets what He tells us; we do. Consequently, we need a "memorial" or an altar to remind us of the promises while waiting for the manifestation.

Reflect
What has God told you during your personal encounters with Him? Have you raised an altar to remind yourself of what He said? How often do you visit your altar?

Pray
Heavenly Father, thank You for access to You. Thank You for revealing Your plans and purposes for my life through the Bible, prayer, and divine encounters with You. May I not forget my personal encounters with You and the things You have shared with me during those times. In Jesus' name I pray. Amen.

Practical Applications
1. Have a quiet time with God daily.
2. Write down whatever God lays on your heart or says to you during your quiet time.
3. Review what He said often until He promise becomes a reality.

12

GODLY COUNSEL

Focus Scripture

I will bless the Lord who has given me counsel.

Psalm 16:7

Daily Scripture Reading: Psalm 1

As humans, our wisdom and knowledge are finite, and we will inevitably encounter issues that will require seeking counsel from others. Proverbs 11:14 says, "Where there is no counsel, the people fall; But in the multitude of counselors there is safety." It is wise to seek counsel from those ahead of us, but we must be selective about the people who have our ears.

Our scripture for today admonishes us not to walk in the counsel of the ungodly. We must receive counsel from people who have a relationship with Jesus and are filled with the Holy Spirit. Receiving godly counsel from Spirit-filled people is wise. However, we must not completely depend on humans as our only source of counsel.

We can receive counsel directly from the Lord through prayer, spending time in the Word, and asking the Holy Spirit to lead and guide us. The Holy Spirit is the Spirit of counsel, and He lives on the inside of those who have received Jesus as their Lord and personal savior. If we are in tune with the Holy Spirit, our ears will hear His voice, telling us the way to go (Isaiah 30:21).

Reflect

Who do you go to when you need advice or counsel? Are the people you seek advice from spirit-filled followers of Jesus? How can you ensure that your counselors give you godly counsel?

Pray

Dear Lord, thank You for the gift of godly people. Help me to seek godly counsel when I need it. Remind me that I have the Spirit of counsel with me all the time, and I can ask Him for advice whenever I need guidance. In Jesus' name I pray. Amen.

Practical Applications

1. Surround yourself with godly people.

2. Ensure you know the source of the wisdom of whoever is giving you advice.

3. Do not share your problems or issues with just anyone. Be cautious about the people you listen to. Remember that words are seeds planted in your heart.

13

WAIT

Focus Scripture

Promise me, O women of Jerusalem, not to awaken love until the time is right.

Song of Solomon 8:4 (NLT)

Daily Scripture Reading: Ecclesiastes 3

In today's world, sex before marriage has become a norm and part of the culture. People are encouraged to have sex as soon as they feel the urge or have a willing, or sometimes unwilling, partner to fulfill their sexual desires. Contrary to what the world thinks, there is an appointed time to have sex.

Sex, just like everything else God created, was made for a purpose and for an appointed time. God created it for procreation and intimacy between a man and a woman in the context of marriage. Sex outside marriage is an abuse of its purpose.

There are consequences of abusing anything, including sex. Premarital sex has physical, emotional, spiritual, psychological, and financial consequences. For these reasons, it is important to wait until the right time to have sex, and that time is in marriage.

God created sex, and He wants us to enjoy sexual intimacy, but we must wait for the right time. Do not awaken sexual desires until the time is right. Focus on other things like school, work, self-improvement, serving/volunteering, spending time with family, and investing in familial and platonic relationships. Sex will be worth the wait.

Reflect

What can you do to keep your sexual desires asleep before marriage? Are there people in your life who awaken your sexual desires? Are there places you visit and things you watch/listen to that stimulate your sexual desires? What can you do to reduce your exposure to those places and things?

Pray

Dear Lord, I learned today that You created sex for our pleasure but only in the context of marriage. Help me wait until marriage to have sex. Give me the grace to focus on the important things in this season of my life. In Jesus' name I pray. Amen.

Practical Applications

1. Make a commitment not to have sex until marriage.
2. Surround yourself with like-minded people who have the same goal.
3. Do not put yourself in compromising situations; run from sexual sin!

14

—◆—

SEX IN MARRIAGE

Focus Scripture

The husband should fulfill his wife's sexual needs, and the wife should fulfill her husband's needs.

1 Corinthians 7:13 (NLT)

Daily Scripture Reading: 1 Corinthians 7

Marriage is not the place to abstain from sex. There are some exceptions, though, such as when a husband and a wife mutually agree to abstain from it for a season of prayer and fasting or in the case of an illness that makes it unsafe for both to have sex. Otherwise, married couples must plan to have lots of sex.

God designed sex as a tool for intimacy between a husband and a wife. Married people are encouraged to have sex often and not leave room for sexual temptations. However, the busyness of life can sometimes force couples to abstain from sex for long periods of time.

This can lead to the temptation of seeking sexual satisfaction from someone or something other than your spouse. Marriage must be honored by all; husbands and wives must be faithful to each other because God will judge those who are immoral and those who commit adultery (Hebrews 13:4 NLT). Do not give place to the devil; commit to making sex a priority in your marriage.

Reflect

How would you rate the sex life between you and your spouse? In what ways can you improve your sex life? What guards do you have in place to remain faithful to your spouse?

Pray

Heavenly Father, thank You for the gift of sex. Please, give me an insatiable desire for my spouse and help me commit to making sex a priority in my marriage. Give me the wisdom to keep my marriage bed alive and to always be enraptured by the love of my spouse. In Jesus' name I pray. Amen.

Practical Applications

1. Have an open conversation with your spouse about how to maintain and/or improve your sexual relationship.

2. Make sex a priority and plan to be intimate with your spouse as often as you both desire.

3. Reduce your commitments to make room for quality time with your spouse. Delegate tasks, hire help if possible, and/or ask for help from friends and family with child care (if applicable).

15

WISDOM

Focus Scripture

The fear of the Lord is the beginning of wisdom, and the knowledge of the Holy One is understanding.

Proverbs 9:10

Daily Scripture Reading: Proverbs 9

Wisdom is knowing what to do per time. A wise person makes the right decisions. A wise person has knowledge and knows how to apply the knowledge they have.

Proverbs 8:11 says wisdom is better than rubies or jewels, and all the things one can desire cannot be compared with wisdom. Also, according to Proverbs 4:5, wisdom is the principal thing. Without wisdom, we cannot accomplish much in life.

We need it to build and establish a house (Proverbs 24:3). A woman needs wisdom to build her home (Proverbs 14:1). A man needs it to lead his family (1 Timothy 3:4-5). We all need wisdom to survive the storms that come with living in a fallen world (Matthew 7:24-25).

Unfortunately, most people lack wisdom. But there is good news! We can ask God for wisdom, just like Solomon asked for it. God gave him wisdom and added riches to it (2 Chronicles 1:7-12). If you lack wisdom in any area of your life, dare to ask God, and He will give it to you (James 1:5).

If you think you are already wise, still ask God for wisdom. You may have earthly, sensual, or demonic wisdom (James 3:15). What we need is divine wisdom. This type that is from above and is pure, peaceable, gentle, willing to yield, full of mercy and good fruits, and is without partiality or hypocrisy (James 3:17).

Reflect
Are you a wise person? Who or where is your wisdom from? Do you fear or revere God and His word?

Pray
Heavenly Father, You are a good Father, and all good and perfect gifts come from You. I lack wisdom in _____ area(s) of my life. Please give me the wisdom I need. Lead and guide me. May I not depend on my own wisdom or that of others. In Jesus' name I pray. Amen.

Practical Applications
1. Choose wise friends. If you walk with the wise, you will be wise, but a companion of fools shall be destroyed (Proverbs 13:20).
2. Obeying God's commandments makes you wise (Proverbs 119:98).
3. If you don't know what to do about a situation, don't muddle through. Ask God for wisdom (James 1:5).

16

UNQUALIFIED

Focus Scripture

But Moses said to God, "Who am I that I should go to Pharaoh, and that I should bring the children of Israel out of Egypt?" So He said, "I will certainly be with you. And this shall be a sign to you that I have sent you: When you have brought the people out of Egypt, you shall serve God on this mountain."

Exodus 3:11-12 NKJV

Daily Scripture Reading: Exodus 3

In today's scripture reading, God sends Moses to deliver the children of Israel from slavery. Moses did not think he was qualified, but that is why God chose him in the first place. God does not use qualified vessels. He uses people who have no qualifications: He neither chooses the mighty nor noble. He chooses weak vessels, like Moses, like you, and me.

The moment we feel qualified for what we think God has called us to do, then we probably are not doing what He wants us to do. "For you see your calling, brethren, that not many wise according to the flesh, not many mighty, not many noble, are called. But God has chosen the foolish things of the world to put to shame the wise, and God has chosen the weak things of the world to put to shame the things which are mighty" (I Corinthians 1:26-27 NKJV).

We may have special gifts that seem to make us feel qualified for the work of God. But having a gift does not automatically mean the Lord can use you. Being called and chosen simply means doing what God tells you to do. Besides, many people have gifts but do not use them for God. God can use what you have to accomplish His purpose, but He does not need what you have. What matters is who sent you. Remembering that keeps us humble.

Reflect

What has God called you to do that you feel unqualified for? What gift(s) do you possess that God can use for His purpose? Do you feel called to use your gifts for God's purposes?

Pray

Almighty God, I am grateful that You can use me as I am. You do not need me to be qualified to do the things You planned for me to do when You created me. Help me not to depend on my abilities, gifts, talents, or lack thereof. Remind me that You are with me and will equip me to do all the things You have assigned me to do. In Jesus' name I pray. Amen.

Practical Applications

1. Write down the gifts you have and ask God to use them for His glory and purpose.

2. Write down things you feel led to do but are unqualified to do by your own strength.

3. Pray for God to use you and your gifts for His glory.

17

— • —

SMALL BEGINNINGS

Focus Scripture
And though you started with little, you will end with much.

Job 8:7

Daily Scripture Reading: Zechariah 4

The beginning of a thing is often difficult, and it requires a lot of patience and hard work. But if we are diligent, the small, insignificant seeds we sow today could grow into a mighty tree and, eventually, a forest tomorrow. Zechariah 4:10 encourages us not to despise the days of small beginnings. It is very easy to despise small beginnings because there is no fruit to show forth. However, the starting stage is the most important part of building anything. This is where the foundations are laid, which is necessary to keep what you are building from falling. Psalm 11:3 says, "If the foundations are destroyed, what can the righteous do?"

Instead of focusing on how small your beginning is, focus on what you are trying to build. Invest your time, efforts, resources, prayers, and attention on what you are building. Take a new pregnancy for instance, the first few weeks are the most crucial because that is when vital organs are formed and when major congenital anomalies occur. The size of the pregnancy is minuscule compared to the internal development. If a pregnant woman despises the first few weeks of her pregnancy, treats her body carelessly, and does not care for the pregnancy or, follow the recommendations of her Obstetrician, complications could arise.

When you start something new, think of it as a new pregnancy. Protect it from harmful external influences that could jeopardize normal growth and development. Cherish, guard, and protect it. Water, feed, and nourish it. Most importantly, pray about what you are building, because unless the Lord builds a house, those who build it labor in vain (Psalm 127:1).

Reflect
What small beginnings in your life are you despising? What can you do to cherish the small steps you have taken in response to what God has called you to do? What can you do to protect your small beginning from harmful external influences?

Pray
Heavenly Father, thank You for Your word today. Help me not to despise the small beginnings of the vision You have committed to my hands. Give me the wisdom to cherish, nourish, and protect my small beginnings. Remind me that You rejoice to see the work begin according to Zechariah 4:10. Help me believe that You, who have begun this work in me, will be faithful to complete it. In Jesus' name I pray. Amen.

Practical Applications
1. Invest time, resources, and prayer into what you are building.
2. Try not to compare your project with what others are building; focus on your project and what God has called you to do.
3. Leave the outcome to God. You can plant and water your project, but God gives the increase.

18

GOD KNOWS, ASK HIM

Focus Scripture

Then Mary said to the angel, "How can this be, since I do not know a man?"

Luke 1:34

Daily Scripture Reading: Genesis 25

In the scripture reading for today, Rebekah had been barren for 20 years. Isaac, her husband, prayed for her to become pregnant and she did. She had a rough pregnancy, and she asked God why. The Lord revealed to her that she was carrying two nations in her womb; one would be stronger than the other, and the older would serve the younger. Though it is unusual for an older son to serve the younger, Rebekah did not ask more questions on how those things would be.

And even though God Himself gave her the revelation, he did not need her help to accomplish His purpose. God's word would have still come to pass regardless of Rebekah and Jacob's schemes to forcefully make it happen. I am not sure how God would have made it happen, but He is all powerful and would have done it.

When God tells us His plans for our lives, it is our responsibility to partner with Him through prayer and obedience to ensure that what He says comes to pass the way He intended. We must not lean on our own understanding. Instead, we must depend on God's guidance and direction on how He wants to achieve His will. Rebekah could have asked God in prayer how He planned to achieve His goal, the same way she had inquired of Him when she was having a difficult pregnancy. Rebekah in her human understanding, assumed that deceiving Isaac was the only way to accomplish what God had spoken to her about her twin children.

We need to learn from Mary, who asked God how the promise would come to pass, when He told her she would conceive and give birth to a son. Then the Lord shared His plan with her and how she would conceive of the Holy Spirit. She did not ask from a place of doubt but from a desire to understand how the promise would unfold. Mary could have assumed how God would achieve His purpose and sinned against Him in the process. But she didn't; she simply asked God.

Reflect

Is there something God has asked you to do or revealed to you that seems impossible or unusual? How did you respond to the instruction? How do you intend to partner with God to accomplish His purpose?

Pray

Heavenly Father, help me to trust in You with all my heart and not lean on my own understanding. I acknowledge You in all my ways, please direct my paths. Whenever I encounter situations that seem impossible, remind me that with You, nothing is impossible. In Jesus' name I pray. Amen.

Practical Applications

1. Trust God to accomplish what He has spoken over your life.
2. Do not sin in an attempt to fulfill God's promise over your life.
3. Stay connected to God for step-by-step directions on how to partner with Him to fulfill His plans for your life.

19

PRAISE THE LORD

Focus Scripture

And she conceived again and bore a son, and said, "Now I will praise the Lord." Therefore she called his name Judah. Then she stopped bearing.

Genesis 29:35

Daily Scripture Reading: Genesis 29

In Genesis 29:31, we see how God opened Leah's womb when He saw that her husband, Jacob, did not love her. However, it took bearing four sons for Leah to finally praise the Lord! Even though it was God who opened her womb in the first place. Sometimes, we wait for God to change our situations before we praise Him. That is not how it should be. We must praise Him regardless of our circumstances. He is worthy of our praise because of who He is, not what He has done or not done for us.

Praising God simply means declaring His names. And when we call on His names, He responds by inhabiting our praises (Psalm 22:3). When He comes down and is enthroned in our praises, what problem or situation can stand against His presence? None! Therein lies our victory. Praise God regardless of what you are going through. This is what invites God to act on your behalf.

I challenge you today, instead of focusing on your problems, focus on praising God. Are you sick? Call on Jehovah Rapha, the Lord who heals. Do you feel unseen? Call on Jehovah El-Roi, the God Who Sees you. Do you need a provision? Praise Jehovah Jireh, the God who provides. Do you need direction for your life? Call on Jehovah-Rohi, the Lord our Shepherd. Are people waging war against you? Praise Jehovah-Sabaoth, the Lord of hosts, and let Him fight on your behalf. Whatever you are going through in life, Jehovah El-Shaddai, the One who is sufficient for the needs of His people, will come to your aid if you call on Him. Let everything that has breath praise the Lord!

Reflect
What situations are you waiting for God to solve before you praise Him? If God does not solve your problem, will you still praise Him? How can you praise God regardless of your situation?

Pray
Heavenly Father, thank You for being all sufficient. You are the I AM and can be whatever I need You to be at any moment. Lord, help me remember this in difficult times. Empower me to choose to praise You regardless of what I go through. I will praise You even if You do nothing else for me because You are worthy of all my praises. In Jesus' name I pray. Amen.

Practical Applications
1. Write down whatever you are going through and look for a name of God that speaks to that situation. Use this resource https://characterbuildingforfamilie s.com/names/ as a guide.
2. Read Psalm 139 and Psalm 145-150 out loud.
3. Don't let your situation determine your praise.

20

KNOW GOD PERSONALLY

Focus Scripture

That I may know Him and the power of His resurrection, and the fellowship of His sufferings, being conformed to His death.

Philippians 3:10

Daily Scripture Reading: Exodus 32

If you really know someone, you know their likes, dislikes, voice, and present and future plans. To know someone, you must spend quality time with them. Knowing God also involves spending quality time with Him in prayer, worship, and reading the Bible. It is impossible to know God without these activities. However, most of us depend solely on other people, like prophets, pastors, and evangelists, to pray for us and teach us the Bible.

Having pastors after God's own heart who can teach us the Word is good and scriptural (Jeremiah 3:15). However, their teachings and prayers should not replace personal prayer and Bible study. After the Word has been preached to us, we need to search the Scriptures daily on our own too (Acts 17:11). We cannot solely depend on what our pastors tell us about God. We must have a personal relationship and encounter with the Almighty such that we know what he likes and dislikes, hear Him when He speaks to us, and obey whatever He commands us to do.

If we do not have a personal relationship with Him, we could end up like the children of Israel who depended on Moses to hear from God. When Moses spent forty days and forty nights with God on Mount Sinai to receive the next set of instructions, the children of Israel could not pray and worship God on their own. They had no direction and did not know what to do. So they created gods to lead them while Moses spent time with God.

Prior to this, God had performed lots of miracles among them through Moses. God delivered them from slavery in Egypt, parted the Red Sea, drowned their enemies in the Red Sea, sustained them in the wilderness with manna and water, and much more. The children of Israel experienced God's mighty acts but did not have a relationship with Him (Psalm 103:7). But God revealed His plans to Moses. He can reveal His plans to us as well if we invest the time to know Him.

Reflect
What is your personal relationship with God like? Do you know how to seek God's face on your own? If your pastor were no longer available, would you still serve God?

Pray
Heavenly Father, thank You because You invite me to know You more deeply. You know me intimately and want me to know You the same way too. Thank You for direct access to You through the finished work of the cross. Help me to make spending time with You a priority so that I may know You personally. In Jesus' name I pray. Amen.

Practical Applications
1. Have a quiet time daily.
2. Learn to read the Bible on your own. Ask the Holy Spirit to explain the scriptures to you.
3. Learn to pray on your own. Desire to hear the voice of God in prayer and Bible study.

21

WHO SENT YOU?

Focus Scripture

So Jesus said to them again, "Peace to you! As the Father has sent Me, I also send you."

John 20:21

Daily Scripture Reading: Judges 6

When someone sends you on an errand, you act on that person's behalf. You act in the person's stead because you are backed by their authority and power. Typically, the sender is someone with authority, power, influence, and is known to the recipients of the message. The messenger is often unknown but may be known in some cases, because of the influence of the sender.

In the scripture reading today, God sent Gideon to deliver the children of Israel from the Midianites. Just like Moses, Gideon felt he was not qualified for the task because his clan was the weakest in Manasseh, and he was the least in his father's house (Judges 6:15). However, God knew he could conquer the Midianites because He was sending him. Not because he was a mighty man of valor! God's backing turned Gideon into one.

God sent every human being to the world for a purpose. This is especially true for the followers of Jesus. He said in John 20:21 (AMP), "as the Father has sent

Me, I also send you [as my representatives]." We were sent into the world for a purpose, and we must do the works of the One who sent us (John 9:4).

Like Gideon, we may sometimes feel inadequate for the task God has sent us to accomplish. However, our inadequacy is irrelevant because we are not sent in our own strength, but in the power and authority of the sender. What truly makes us inadequate for the task is our failure to respond when God sends us. Our response should be "Here I am, send me" (Isaiah 6:8). As long as we are doing what He wants us to do, He promises to be with us always, even to the end of the world (Matthew 28:20).

Reflect
Have you ever acted on behalf of someone powerful? How did that make you feel? Think about acting on behalf of the One who created the heavens and the earth. What wouldn't you be able to accomplish in His strength?

Pray
Heavenly Father, I know You sent me here for a purpose. May my response be "Here I am, send me." Remove every doubt from my heart. Help me remember that You will never leave or forsake me as I do what You have called me to do. In Jesus' name I pray. Amen.

Practical Applications
1. Write down what God has sent you to do.
2. Take practical steps to accomplish the task(s).
3. Remind yourself as you complete the task(s) that you were sent by God and must depend on Him for directions and instructions for the mission.

22

—— • ——

AS THE LORD COMMANDS

Focus Scripture

Samuel said, "Which does the Lord prefer: obedience or offerings and sacrifices? It is better to obey Him than to sacrifice the best sheep to Him."

1 Samuel 15:22 (GNT)

Daily Scripture Reading: 1 Samuel 15

Obeying God can be difficult at times, especially as He often calls us to do things that we cannot do by our own strength. Sometimes His instructions do not make sense, but this should not be surprising because God's ways and thoughts are not like ours. Whenever we try to understand His commandments with our finite minds, we fall into the trap of doing what makes sense to us instead of simply obeying Him.

In 1 Samuel 15:2-3, God gave specific instructions to Saul to destroy everything in Amalek. But Saul spared Agag, the best sheep, oxen, fatlings, lambs, and all the good things in the land. He spared the best sheep and oxen to sacrifice them all to God. However, the Lord's instructions were clear: destroy everything.

There have possibly been times in our lives when God gave us instructions that seemed illogical. The we "modify" them and do what we think is best.

Partial obedience is still disobedience. When God tells you to destroy everything, destroy everything. Don't leave room for rationalization. God is pleased when we obey Him, even when we do not fully understand the rationale behind His instructions. Trusting that He will never instruct us to do things that will harm us will make obedience to Him easier.

Reflect

Do you trust that God is for you and wants what is best for you? What areas of your life do you not trust in God's goodness? What have you done in disobedience because you did not see the benefit of obeying God?

Pray

Heavenly Father, thank You because Your thoughts towards me are good and not evil. I trust that Your commandments are for my benefit, and You will never ask me to do anything that will harm me. Help me to trust and obey You even when I don't understand Your instructions. In Jesus' name I pray. Amen.

Practical Applications

1. Read Jeremiah 29:11 and Proverbs 3:5.
2. Remind yourself daily that God loves you and wants the best for you.
3. Pray for grace and strength to obey His commandments.

23

FORGIVENESS

Focus Scripture

Then Peter came to Him and said, "Lord, how often shall my brother sin against me, and I forgive him? Up to seven times?" Jesus said to him, "I do not say to you, up to seven times, but up to seventy times seven."

Matthew 18:21-22

Daily Scripture Reading: Matthew 18

To forgive is to let go of the hurt and pain of a wrong done to you. Forgiveness does not mean the offender is absolved of the consequences of their actions. Instead, it means that we acknowledge a person's offense and its effect on us, we let go of our anger or disappointment, and we leave vengeance to God.

Although forgiveness is hard, it is not impossible. When we think of it as a command that requires obedience, it becomes easier. And understanding that our decision to withhold forgiveness from a person has consequences will help us forgive quickly and as often as needed up to seven times seventy times!

If we decide not to forgive those who have offended us, God will also not forgive our sins (Matthew 6:15). Remember that we have all sinned and fallen short of His glory (Romans 3:23). So we need His forgiveness, too! If He does not forgive our sins, we cannot relate with Him because God is holy and cannot stand sin.

Our sin separates us from Him and hides His face from us (Isaiah 59:2). And when we pray while we are living in sin, he will not hear or answer because the prayer of a sinner is an abomination to Him (Proverbs 15:8). Without a relationship with God, our life here on earth is meaningless. Choose to forgive; your relationship with the Almighty depends on it.

Reflect

How would you rate your ability to forgive on a scale of one to ten? Is there anyone in your life that you are withholding forgiveness from? How does knowing that God's forgiveness of your sins depends on your willingness to forgive others affect your approach to forgiveness?

Pray

Heavenly Father, I confess that I have withheld forgiveness from people who have hurt me. I know unforgiveness is a sin, and it affects my relationship with You. Forgive my sins as I forgive those who have sinned against me. Give me the grace to forgive like the offense never happened. In Jesus' name I pray. Amen.

Practical Applications

1. Search your heart to identify the people whom you are withholding forgiveness from. Write down their names and their offenses (be specific).

2. In prayer, mention their names and what they have done, and declare that you forgive them.

3. Repeat the prayers as many times as you need until you no longer feel hurt or angry because of their sin.

24

LOVE YOUR ENEMIES

Focus Scripture

If your enemy is hungry, give him bread to eat; And if he is thirsty, give him water to drink; For so you will heap coals of fire on his head, and the Lord will reward you.

Proverbs 25:21-22

Daily Scripture Reading: Luke 6

Jesus instructs us in Luke 6:27-28, to love our enemies, do good to those who hate us, bless those who curse us, and pray for those who mistreat us. It took me a while to really understand the purpose of loving my enemies until recently. Prior to this new revelation, I would quote Proverbs 25:21-22, and reassure myself that loving my enemies would heap coals of fire on their heads. In my limited understanding, I assumed that the heaping coals of fire meant punishing them for their sins. But that is not why Jesus instructed us to love our enemies.

The ultimate purpose of that instruction is to lead them to repentance. Heaping coals of fire on our enemies' heads means repaying the evil done to us with good. This gesture leads our enemies to repentance. God desires that no one should perish but that all people would come to repentance, including our enemies (2 Peter 3:9).

Think about our relationship with God. Christ loved us while we were still His enemies. While we were yet sinners, He died for us (Romans 5:8). His kindness that has led us to repentance and a relationship with Him (Romans 2:4). As followers of Jesus, this is our model: kindness to our enemies even before they realize their sins. This is what it means to heap coals of fire on their heads, and that is what leads them to repentance.

Reflect

Do you have enemies? How can you practically love them? What would you do if loving your enemies does not lead to their repentance?

Pray

Dear Lord, thank You for loving me when I was your enemy. I realize that Your unconditional love is what led me to repentance. Help me to follow in Your footsteps by loving my enemies as You did. In Jesus' name I pray. Amen.

Practical Applications

1. Write down the names of your enemies.

2. List three things that you can do to show your love to them and do them.

3. Be prepared that it may take multiple acts of kindness and love to bring your enemies to repentance, so do not give up. And remember that you will be rewarded by the Lord.

25

PRAYERS OF INTERCESSION

Focus Scripture

Who is he who condemns? It is Christ who died, and furthermore is also risen, who is even at the right hand of God, who also makes intercession for us.

Romans 8:34

Daily Scripture Reading: Nehemiah 1

Intercession means praying on behalf of another person, group of people, or nation(s). Prayers of intercession are important, especially in cases of repentance from sin and reconciliation to God. Except by some miraculous intervention, it is impossible for people born in sin, whose minds have been blinded by the gods of this world to see the need for repentance (2 Corinthians 4:4). We cannot expect people who do not think they have sinned against God to repent, so we must intercede for them by asking the Lord to open their eyes.

The Bible is filled with multiple examples of intercession for repentance. Stephen prayed that God would forgive the sins of Saul and his murderers (Acts 7:60). Moses prayed that God would forgive the idolatry of the children of Israel (Exodus 32:31-35). Jesus prayed for the forgiveness of our sins on the cross (Luke 23:34). Ultimately, these prayers were answered, as Saul became a believer (Acts 9:1-19), the children of Israel repented from their idolatry (Exodus 33:13-17), one thief on the cross repented (Luke 23:42-43), and those who trust in the finished work of Jesus now have a relationship with the Father (Romans 10:9-10).

There is a heavenly reward awaiting those who intercede for others. Crowns of glory await us in heaven for our prayers of intercession. Luke 15:1 says heaven rejoices when one sinner repents. Don't you think the person responsible for the sinner's repentance will be rewarded? Absolutely! Let us take up the mantle of intercession, and pray until we see the fruit of repentance in people and our nation(s).

Reflect
Are there people in your life who need to be reconciled to God? Do you pray for their repentance regularly? Have you seen the fruit of your prayers?

Pray
Dear Lord, thank You for making intercession for me to be reconciled with the Father when I was still a sinner. Thank You for helping me recognize that the repentance of people and nations are tied to my prayers of intercession for them. Show me the people that I need to pray for and give me the grace to intercede on their behalf. Help me not to be discouraged when I don't see the immediate fruit of my prayers. In Jesus' name I pray. Amen.

Practical Applications
1. Write down the names of family members, friends, and coworkers who do not have a relationship with Jesus.
2. Pray for them regularly.
3. Do not stop praying for them until you see the fruit of your prayers, which is their reconciliation to God.

26

DO YOU UNDERSTAND?

Focus Scripture

Wisdom is the principal thing; Therefore get wisdom. And in all your getting, get understanding.

Proverbs 4:7

Daily Scripture Reading: Psalm 119

I made it a personal goal to encourage as many people as possible to read the Bible daily. Many believers do not read the Bible for a lot of reasons. Some often cite the overwhelming volume of the Bible, not knowing where to begin, and a lack of understanding when they read, among others.

I believe a lack of understanding when reading it is one of the major deterrents to reading the Holy Book. This makes sense because the Bible is the inspired word of God, and it cannot be understood except the Holy Spirit of God gives us understanding. If we want to understand the Bible when we read it, we must ask the Holy Spirit to open the eyes of our understanding (Psalm 119:18).

You can also ask someone to explain the word to you. Jeremiah 29:11 says that God has given us pastors according to His heart who can feed us with wisdom and understanding. We see an example in Acts 8:26-37 where an Ethiopian eunuch attempted to read the Bible but did not understand what he was reading.

Then the Holy Spirit led Philip to meet up with him to explain the Scriptures to him.

Philip's explanation of the Scriptures led the Ethiopian eunuch to salvation. Perhaps, your salvation and deliverance in certain areas of life are linked to an understanding of the word. Don't just read the word this year, seek to understand what you are reading and apply it to your life.

Reflect
Do you read the Bible daily? If not, what deters you? If yes, do you understand what you read?

Pray
Heavenly Father, open my eyes that I may behold wondrous things out of Your law. Holy Spirit, please help me understand the word when I read it. Make the Bible come alive in my mind and help me understand what I read. Lead me to pastors after Your heart who will feed me with wisdom and understanding. In Jesus' name I pray. Amen.

Practical Applications
1. Commit to reading the Bible daily, whether you understand what you read or not.
2. Before you read it, pray and ask the Holy Spirit to give you understanding.
3. Ask someone you trust (like your pastor) to explain the word to you as needed.

27

BENEFITS OF GOD'S WORD

Focus Scripture

Search from the book of the Lord, and read: not one of these shall fail; not one shall lack her mate. For My mouth has commanded it, and His Spirit has gathered them.

Isaiah 34:16

Daily Scripture Reading: Psalm 19

When people are encouraged to do something, they often want to know how it will benefit them. Sometimes, the perceived benefits can be a motivator. Since I have been encouraging people to read the Bible daily, I thought it necessary to share some benefits of reading God's word. Below are ten of the numerous benefits of reading the word:

1. The word of God provides restoration and refreshment for the soul (Psalm 19:7).

2. It gives wisdom to those who lack it (Psalm 19:7).

3. It brings joy to the heart (Psalm 19:8).

4. The word of God enlightens the eyes and gives insight for living (Psalm 19:8 [NLT]).

5. It provides warnings (Psalm 19:11).

6. It gives life (Proverbs 4:22).

7. It gives healing and health to the body (Proverbs 4:22).

8. It provides healing (Psalm 107:20).

9. It leads to deliverance from destruction (Psalm 107:20).

10. There is a great reward for obeying the word of God (Psalm 19:11).

Reflect:
Besides the ones listed above, what are the other benefits you can gain from reading the word of God? What benefits are you hoping to derive from it? Would you still read the word of God if there were no tangible benefits?

Pray
Heavenly Father, give me an insatiable desire for Your word. May I experience all the benefits of reading Your word. In Jesus' name I pray. Amen.

Practical Applications
1. Commit to reading the word daily.
2. For each verse or chapter of the Bible you read, write down something you learn and can apply to your life.
3. Share what you have learned with others.

28

HEAR AND OBEY

Focus Scripture

So then, anyone who hears these words of mine and obeys them is like a wise man who built his house on rock.

Matthew 7:24

Daily Scripture Reading: Matthew 7

All Scripture is inspired by God, and it is useful for instruction, conviction of sin, correction, restoration to obedience, and for training in righteousness (2 Timothy 3:16). Reading the Bible is like God speaking directly to us. For us to enjoy the benefits of the word, we must do what God says in it.

James 1:22 admonishes us to be both hearers and doers of God's word. It is in hearing and doing His word that we are blessed. Jesus said in Matthew 7:24 that anyone who hears and obeys the word is like a wise man who built his house upon a rock. Anyone who hears and does not obey is like a foolish man who built his house on sand (Matthew 7:24). When we hear and obey the word, we will be like a tree planted by the rivers of water that is fruitful in its season, whose leaves do not wither, and is prosperous in everything (Psalm 1:2-4). We will also have success if we obey (Joshua 1:8).

Hearing and obeying the word can be likened to having faith. The first part of faith is hearing the word, while the second part is obedience. The two must exist together. Faith is the currency of the spirit, without which it is impossible to please God (Hebrews 11:6).

Reflect

What has God told you to do through His word and personal encounters with Him? What is stopping you from doing them? What practical steps of faith can you take to be a doer of the word?

Pray

Heavenly Father, thank You for Your word. Please, help me to be a hearer and doer of Your word. In Jesus' name I pray. Amen.

Practical Applications

1. Commit to reading the word daily.
2. Meditate on what you have read day and night.
3. Find ways to practically apply God's word to your life.

29

ANGER

Focus Scripture

If you become angry, do not let your anger lead you into sin, and do not stay angry all day.

Ephesians 4:26 (GNT)

Daily Scripture Reading: Ephesians 4

Anger is an emotion that everyone will experience at some point in their lives. We can be angry about injustice, sin, and/or ungodly behavior. It is okay to be angry, but it is never okay to give the devil a foothold in our lives because of it. Thus, how we manage our anger is important.

The Bible gives us clear instructions on how to manage anger when it arises. First, we are not to get angry too quickly (Ecclesiastes 7:9). Second, we ought to forgive on time when we are angry and not let the sun go down on our anger (Ephesians 4:26). The longer we stay angry, the more likely we are to hold a grudge, harbor resentment, and cultivate bitterness (Ephesians 4:27).

When anger arises, pray. God can reveal whether or not our anger is justified in prayer. In Genesis 4:6-7, Cain was angry because God rejected his offering and accepted Abel's offering. Cain did not give a good offering to begin with, so God's rejection was justified, and he had no reason to be angry.

When anger arises, discuss the issue with the parties concerned. You may have misunderstood the person's actions and may have been angry unjustly. Be mindful that whoever is angry with his brother without a cause shall be in danger of judgment (Matthew 5:22). If your anger is justified, resolve the issue to avoid resentment, bitterness, murder, and sin.

When anger arises, pray for the people or things that caused it. Also, pray for yourself so that it can be released from your heart. Anger dwells in the heart of fools (Ecclesiastes 7:9).

Reflect
What makes you angry? How have you managed your anger in the past? Did your anger cause you to sin? How can you prevent sin when you are angry?

Pray
Heavenly Father, give me a heart that is accommodating and not easily angered. When I am angry, help me to forgive quickly. I never want the sun to go down on my anger. Give me the grace to pray when I am angry and the grace to resolve issues with the parties involved. Help me to keep my heart free of anger, bitterness, and resentment that I may worship You in spirit and in truth. In Jesus' name I pray. Amen.

Practical Applications
1. Be honest about your emotions; acknowledge your anger.
2. Acknowledge the cause.
3. Pray about it and the circumstances leading to your anger. Take steps to resolve the issues.

30

HELP

Focus Scripture

My help comes from the Lord, who made heaven and earth.

Psalm 121:2

Daily Scripture Reading: Psalm 121

No one in life achieves anything without help. In fact, we cannot achieve or amount to anything without the help of God and people. From the moment we are born, we need help to breathe, eat, maintain hygiene, and survive. The parents of a newborn, especially the mother, ensure the survival of the child by helping them do things they cannot do on their own. Without the help of people, babies, no matter how talented or gifted they are, will not survive to become all that God created them to be.

There is no such thing as a self-made person. We all need help. Help can come in the form of provision, protection, love, care, counsel, direction, guidance, opportunities, refuge, strength, deliverance, and preservation, to name a few. Although God has placed people in our lives to help us, at the end of the day, our help comes from Him. A mother and father who are supposed to be a child's first helpers can forsake the child, but God said He will never leave us nor forsake us. He also said He will be our helper (Psalm 27:10). How reassuring! If you have lost your mother and/or father, don't worry. You're not without help. God will send you help from the sanctuary and strengthen you from Zion (Psalm 20:2).

Like Moses, He will send Pharaoh's daughter to adopt you (Exodus 2:9-10). Like Esther, He will send a Mordecai to care for you in your father's stead (Esther 2:7).

When we grow up and are not directly cared for by our parents, He still sends us help through people who are not even related to us. he can help us by giving us favor with people. People in authority will like and choose to help us. After Esther was raised by Mordecai and she moved to the palace, Hegai helped her, and she was favored by King Ahasuerus in the end (Esther 2:8-9,17). After Moses fled Egypt to Midian, Jethro, who later became his father-in-law, helped him (Exodus 2:16-22).

When we have exhausted the help of people, God Himself will help us through the ministry of the Holy Spirit, the best Helper (John 14:26, Psalm 54:4, Isaiah 41:10-13, Psalm 46:5). We are never without help. In whatever form help comes our way, may we never forget that our help comes from the Lord who made heaven and earth (Psalm 121:2).

Reflect
How has God helped you? In what ways have people been helpful to you? What can you do to help other people?

Pray
Heavenly Father, thank You for being my source of help. I know my help comes from You, the maker of heaven and earth. Thank You for bringing destiny helpers into my life. Open my eyes to recognize the helpers You send my way and not to despise them. In Jesus' name I pray. Amen.

Practical Applications
1. Write down the ways God has helped you from birth to date, and thank Him.
2. Write down the names of people God has used to help you thus far and send them a "thank you" message.
3. Write down the things you need help with and thank God for sending you help.

31

— • —

EYES ON JESUS

Focus Scripture

I have told you all this so that you may have peace in me. Here on earth you will have many trials and sorrows. But take heart, because I have overcome the world.

John 16:33

Daily Scripture Reading: John 14

Many people think that being a follower of Jesus is a walk in the park, but it is not. While there are countless benefits of being a believer, there are also challenges that come because of our relationship with Jesus. It is good to know that as Christians, perilous times will come, especially in these last days (2 Timothy 3:1). We must be aware so that when the storms of life hit, we will be prepared to weather them.

The beautiful thing about being a believer is that we do not have to weather the storms of life on our own. We have a Savior who has won the battles and weathered all the storms for us already. All we need to do is look to Him, the author and finisher of our faith (Hebrews 12:2).

How Apostle Peter accomplished the impossible - walked on water - as long as his eyes were fixed on Jesus comes to mind (Matthew 14:29). When he looked at the boisterous wind around him, he began to sink (Matthew 14:30). If Peter had kept his eyes on Jesus, who knows how much longer he would have walked on water? There is a great lesson here. Keep your eyes on Jesus! Don't look at the storm, trial, difficulty, or challenge. They will make you afraid, and you will begin to sink. Keep your eyes fixed on Jesus.

Reflect

What challenges have you faced or are facing now? How did you overcome your previous challenges? How can you keep your eyes on Jesus instead of on your current challenges?

Pray

Dear Jesus, help me fix my eyes on You no matter what goes on around me. Even if the earth is moved, the mountains thrown into the sea, and the oceans roar, keep my eyes on You. Remind my heart to be still and know that the Lord of hosts is with me and will be my refuge in the storm. In Jesus' name I pray. Amen.

Practical Applications

1. Read Psalm 46 aloud.
2. Keep your eyes on the word and obey. Jesus told Peter to "come." Peter obeyed but somewhere along the line, he gave in to doubts (Matthew 14:31). Do not doubt.
3. Ask Jesus to save you from sinking. When Peter was afraid and was beginning to sink, he asked Jesus to save him, and immediately Jesus stretched out His hand and caught him (Matthew 14:30-31). Ask Jesus for help.

32

TESTIMONIES

Focus Scripture

I have not hidden Your righteousness within my heart; I have declared Your faithfulness and Your salvation; I have not concealed Your lovingkindness and Your truth from the great assembly.

Psalm 40:10

Daily Scripture Reading: Psalm 40

God has done so many wonderful things for us that cannot be recounted in order, because they are just so much (Psalm 40:5). A testimony is simply sharing publicly what God has done for us. Testimonies must be shared publicly and not hidden in our hearts (Psalm 40:10). However, people, for whatever reason, often shy away from sharing their testimonies in public. Perhaps because some testimonies are "shameful" or "embarrassing". There is no such thing as shameful or embarrassing testimony!

Sharing our testimonies with others benefits us and the hearers. It encourages the listeners to know that there is someone else going through similar issues and that there is no temptation that every temptation is common to the human experience (1 Corinthians 10:13). The hearers of our testimony will know that the God who came through for us will come through for them as well, because the Lord shows no partiality (Acts 10:34). Sharing our testimonies builds the faith of those who hear them (Romans 10:17). Our testimonies counsel others on how to overcome similar challenges and provide direction on how to get similar results (Psalm 119:24).

The next time God does something for you, don't keep quiet about it. Shout it on the mountain top and declare His praises (Isaiah 42:11-12). That is how we overcome the devil – by the blood of the Lamb and by the word of our testimonies (Revelation 12:11).

Reflect
Do you have testimonies that you are ashamed of or embarrassed to share? What makes it embarrassing or shameful to share? What can you do to set yourself free from the "shame" of your testimony?

Pray
Dear Heavenly Father, thank You for all You have done for me! If I were to list them all, it would take me an eternity. Give me the boldness and courage to share the things You have done for me publicly. I nail the shame of what You delivered me from on the cross and choose to declare Your wondrous works to anyone who would listen. As I share my testimonies with others, may they be blessed, encouraged, strengthened, and counseled. And may my testimony be permanent. In Jesus' name I pray. Amen.

Practical Applications
1. Attempt to write down everything God has done for you from birth to date.
2. Write down the "embarrassing" or "shameful" testimonies, and list why they are shameful and embarrassing.
3. Decide to share them with someone or publicly as you are led. Remember that you are not your past. If God has delivered you from something shameful, you are not that thing anymore. You have a new identity in Christ. Don't stay bound by keeping your testimony to yourself! It will bless someone. Share it.

33

— ◦ —

OTHERS

Focus Scripture

Let each of you look out not only for his own interests, but also for the interests of others.

Philippians 2:4

Daily Scripture Reading: Mark 6

Soul care is a necessity. Jesus wants us to care for ourselves, but not at the expense of others. As we care for ourselves, He expects us to think about and minister to the needs of others. We all have needs, but there is always someone with a greater need than ourselves.

A mother and her baby come to mind. Every mother will tell you that they need sleep and rest at night. But when their baby wakes up to be fed and cared for in the middle of the night, they set aside their need for sleep and minister to the needs of their child. God expects that from us, too, not just with our biological children or family members, but with strangers in need of help.

In Mark 6:30-32, Jesus advised His disciples to pull away to a deserted place to rest and minister to their personal needs. But on their way, they met people with a greater need, the need of a Shepherd (Mark 6:34). The disciples paused, per Jesus' instructions, to meet the needs of others (Mark 6:35-44). After ministering to the needs of the people, they continued their journey to refresh themselves (Mark 6:45).

Next time you're on your way to meet your needs, think about the needs of others, too. When taking your needs to God in prayer, and you remember a sister or brother who has a need, pause and take a minute to pray for them. As you work to meet your basic needs for food, clothing, and shelter, think about others and help them meet their basic needs as well. As you do that, Jesus will also interrupt His plans to meet your needs.

In Mark 6:46-47, Jesus was on the mountain praying, meeting His spiritual need of communion with the Father. Then He saw that His disciples were in need and struggling to row their boat as the wind was contrary (Mark 6:48). Jesus took a break from meeting His own need to help His disciples, and He saved them from potentially perishing in the sea (Mark 6:51). Jesus knows and sees your needs. If you care about the needs of others, He will care for yours as well.

Reflect
What are your needs? What can you do to meet the needs of others as you trust God to meet yours? How does helping someone in need prevent you from meeting your own needs?

Pray
Dear Heavenly Father, thank You because through You and the finished work of Jesus on the cross, all my needs are met. Help me not to just be concerned about my own needs but to be concerned about the needs of others as well. I know that You will care for me as I care for the needs of others. In Jesus' name I pray. Amen.

Practical Applications
1. Write down your needs.
2. Write down the needs of others in your church, family, community, nation, and place of employment.
3. Write down what you can do to meet the needs listed in number two and do them.

34

CREATED FOR GOOD WORKS

Focus Scripture

For we are His workmanship, created in Christ Jesus for good works, which God prepared beforehand that we should walk in them.

Ephesians 2:10

Daily Scripture Reading: Ephesians 2

As believers in Jesus, our goal is to make heaven and be reunited with our Lord and Savior. However, while we are still on earth, God expects our impact to be felt by those around us. According to our key scripture for today, God has preordained good works for us to accomplish while we are on earth.

There was a woman named Dorcas (also known as Tabitha) in the Bible, who was full of good works and charitable deeds (Acts 9:36). When she died, people mourned her death and spoke about all the good works she did while she was alive (Acts 9:39). Just like Dorcas, every believer must have good works that can speak for them when they are gone.

To accomplish the good works that God has prepared for us to complete, we must be thoroughly equipped (2 Timothy 3:17). We become equipped by reading and studying the word of God and following the leading of the Holy Spirit (2 Timothy 2:15). Think of the Bible as a manual for the good works that

God has prepared for you and decide to follow the directions written in it for you.

Reflect
What good works have you accomplished so far in your time on earth? What good work can you do to better the lives of those around you? What would people miss about you when you are gone?

Pray
Heavenly Father, thank You for preparing good works for me to complete. Help me to discover the good works You have prepared for me to do. Give me the grace and courage to step out in faith to accomplish them. In Jesus' name I pray. Amen.

Practical Applications
1. Commit to reading the Bible daily; that is how you will become equipped for good works.
2. Write down the good work you can do for people in your community, church, school, or place of employment.
3. Prayerfully take steps to accomplish the good works you have written down.

35

— • —

MINISTRY OF RECONCILIATION

Focus Scripture

Now all things are of God, who has reconciled us to Himself through Jesus Christ, and has given us the ministry of reconciliation.

2 Corinthians 5:18

Daily Scripture Reading: 2 Corinthians 5

Reconciliation means becoming friendly with someone again. Due to the fall of man in the Garden of Eden, we were separated from God, and we became His enemies (Genesis 3:23). However, through the death and resurrection of Jesus, we have been reconciled to God and are friends with Him again (Romans 5:10). Hallelujah!

If you are a believer in Jesus, we have all been given the ministry of reconciliation. Jesus had one purpose in life, and that was to reconcile us to God. He fulfilled His calling by reconciling people in His day to the Father. Before Jesus left the earth, He committed the ministry of reconciliation to His disciples, and they reconciled others to God as well. The ministry of reconciliation has continued to date.

As present-day followers of Jesus, the buck stops with us. We must also reconcile others to God, just as Christ did for us. The method of reconciliation will look different for everyone. Some will reconcile others through their gifts/talents, prayer, evangelism, giving, healing, feeding the poor, loving outcasts/people who are unloved, and most importantly, living a life that reflects a relationship with God.

Reflect

Are you grateful to have a restored relationship with God? Has anyone been reconciled back to God through you? What can you do to begin your ministry of reconciliation?

Pray

Dear Lord, thank You for reconciling me to my heavenly Father. Thank You for the price You paid for my salvation. Help me to share what You have done for me with others who are yet to be reconciled to God. In Jesus' name I pray. Amen.

Practical Applications

1. Write down the date you were reconciled to God.

2. Write down the names of people in your life who need to be reconciled to Him.

3. Prayerfully consider the methods you can use to reconcile those people to God.

36

BE HOLY

Focus Scripture

Speak to all the congregation of the children of Israel and say to them: 'You shall be holy, for I the Lord your God am holy.'

Leviticus 19:2

Daily Scripture Reading: Leviticus 19

Hebrews 12:14 urges us to pursue peace with all people and holiness, without which no one will see the Lord.

To be holy means being set apart, consecrated, sacred, and without evil, sin, or blemish. God is holy, and as His children, He expects us to be holy, too (Leviticus 19:2). When we are holy, we are completely devoted to God, perfect in goodness and righteousness, and without sin.

As humans living in a fallen and broken world, our natural tendency is not holiness. But we can become holy just as our Father in heaven is holy. We become holy when we obey His commandments. Contrary to popular beliefs, His commandments are not burdensome (1 John 5:3).

When we read the Old Testament, we can easily become overwhelmed by all the rules and laws. However, Jesus summarized all the laws and commandments into two simple commandments: love God and love your neighbor as yourself

(Matthew 22:37-40). If we love God, we will keep His commandments (1 John 5:3). If we keep His commandments, we will become holy (1 Peter 1:14-16). With God's help, holiness is possible.

Reflect

Are you living a holy life? What are you doing that prevents you from being holy? In what ways can you practice holiness, just as God is holy?

Pray

Heavenly Father, thank You for giving me the capacity to be holy just as You are. I recognize that You will never instruct me to do anything that You have not given me the ability to do. Because of the finished work of the cross, I know that I can live a holy life. Help me to yield to the leading of the Holy Spirit and to live a life that is holy and acceptable to You. In Jesus' name I pray. Amen.

Practical Applications

1. Determine to love God with all your heart, soul, and mind (Deuteronomy 6:5, Matthew 22:37).
2. Commit to loving your neighbor as yourself (Matthew 22:39).
3. Repent as soon as you fall short of this standard (Romans 3:23).

37

EXAMPLES

Focus Scripture

Now all these things happened to them as examples, and they were written for our admonition, upon whom the ends of the ages have come.

1 Corinthians 10:11

Daily Scripture Reading: 1 Corinthians 10

I am sure you have heard the expression "there is nothing new under the sun" quoted from Ecclesiastes 1:9. There is nothing you are going through that someone somewhere has not already gone through. You can have a group of people who experience the same challenges, but some successfully overcome them while others are defeated. The difference is in how they approached their challenges.

Sometimes, when we are faced with difficulties, we think our experiences are unique to us. That is untrue. Scripture and history are filled with examples of people who have experienced the same things that we have experienced, are experiencing, or will experience in the future. God, in His mercy, has inspired people to document their experiences in Scripture and books so we will never be without guidance or direction.

It behooves us to read the Bible and whatever resources we are led to read, identify situations in our lives that others have experienced, and learn from how they handled those situations. In some cases, we will learn what to do, and in other cases, we will learn what not to do. The bottom line is, you can learn from the experiences of others and not have to reinvent the wheel.

As you read the Word of God, you will realize that whatever you are going through is not new. Other people have similar experiences. The idea is that as we read the happenings of the lives of others, we can learn from how they overcame and apply some of their strategies to our own issues. If you cannot find what you are going through in Scripture, you will definitely find a key wisdom applicable to your situation. Don't stop reading the Word!

Reflect
What challenges are you facing currently? Can you identify people in the Bible who faced similar challenges? How did they handle it? What was the outcome of their strategy? Would applying the same strategy they applied yield a positive outcome for you? Is there a trusted friend you can share your challenges with?

Pray
Heavenly Father, I thank You for the gift of Your word. I thank You that You have provided solutions for everything that I will ever face in Scripture. You have also placed people strategically in my life to help me with challenging situations. Help me to seek counsel from Your word and godly people. Remind me that I am never alone and that You are always with me to help me navigate whatever challenges I encounter. I trust You to lead and guide me to specific scriptures and people who can help me navigate life's challenges. In Jesus' name I pray. Amen.

Practical Applications
1. Write down whatever challenges you are facing currently.
2. Identify and write down 5-10 Scriptures that specifically address your current situation. Read them aloud multiple times a day to yourself.
3. Pray about your challenges and share them with someone who could pray with you.

38

CUSTOMS AND TRADITIONS

Focus Scripture

Then the Pharisees and scribes asked Him, "Why do Your disciples not walk according to the tradition of the elders, but eat bread with unwashed hands?"

Mark 7:5

Daily Scripture Reading: Mark 7

Customs are practices common to a particular group of people. Traditions are inherited ideas, thoughts, actions, or behaviors passed down verbally or by example from generation to generation. Customs and traditions are good, but there must be a firm boundary between keeping customs and traditions versus obeying God's commandments.

Any custom or tradition that is contrary to the word of God must be abandoned. When we become saved, we must abandon our customs and traditions if they do not align with His commandments and adopt the customs and traditions of the Kingdom of God. We must not lay aside the commandment of God to uphold man-made customs and traditions (Mark 7:8-9).

Some customs and traditions are not bad in the grand scheme of things, but are they beneficial? (1 Corinthians 6:12). Would keeping those customs and traditions make people confused about where you stand in your faith? Before you hold fast to any custom or tradition, research its origin, purpose, and whether or not it aligns with God's commandments.

Reflect

What customs and traditions are you practicing that were passed down from your parents or grandparents? Are those practices contrary to God's commandments? What new traditions have you adopted since becoming a follower of Jesus?

Pray

Heavenly Father, thank You for adopting me into Your family. Help me to learn and take up the customs and traditions of my new family. I repent for practicing traditions that are contrary to Your word. In Jesus' name I pray. Amen.

Practical Applications

1. Know what you're doing and why you're doing it.
2. Commit to stop doing things that are displeasing to God in the name of keeping up with traditions.
3. Read the Word regularly so you can adopt the customs and traditions of the Kingdom.

39

TIMES OF IGNORANCE

Focus Scripture

Truly, these times of ignorance God overlooked, but now commands everyone everywhere to repent.

Acts 17:30

Daily Scripture Reading: Leviticus 4

The principles of the physical realm are a reflection of the principles of the spiritual realm. In the physical realm, we are bound by laws and are expected to obey them, regardless of whether we know what they are or not. If you visit a country, and the law of that country is not to drive after 8 PM, but you are ignorant of the law, that does not exempt you from being held accountable for your actions if you disobey. If you are in that country, you are expected to know and obey the laws governing it.

The same is true in the spiritual realm. There are laws and principles that govern the activities of the realm, and you are not exempt from the consequences of disobedience just because you are ignorant of the laws. If you disobey the law, there will be consequences. Before we become saved, we do things that are not pleasing to God due to ignorance. But when we become saved, we are expected to acquaint ourselves with the laws of God and obey them.

As you become familiar with the laws of the Kingdom of God and realize your shortcomings, repentance is required. God is merciful and will overlook the days of our ignorance, but once we know the truth, we must repent (Acts 17:30). Anyone who knows the right thing and does not do it is committing a sin (James 4:17).

Reflect

What have you done in the past that you did not realize was sinful? How did you respond when you realized those actions were sinful? What are you doing to become familiar with laws of God so you can obey them?

Pray

Heavenly Father, thank You for overlooking my sin when I was ignorant of your commandments. Thank You for Your grace and mercy in not giving me what I deserve. Thank You for making a way in Jesus for the forgiveness of my past, present, and future sins. Help me to become familiar with the laws of Your Kingdom and to obey them. In Jesus' name I pray. Amen.

Practical Applications

1. Repent of any sin you committed in your days of ignorance.

2. Read the word daily to become familiar with the laws of God's Kingdom.

3. Commit to obeying God's commandments.

40

INTERNATIONAL WOMEN'S DAY

Focus Scripture

Charm is deceitful and beauty is passing, but a woman who fears the Lord, shall be praised.

Proverbs 31:30

Daily Scripture Reading: Proverbs 31

The United States and some other countries recognize March as Women's History Month. March 8th is often celebrated as International Women's Day globally. Happy International Women's Day to all women around the globe (if you are a woman reading this on March 8th). We see your impact on our world and are grateful for you.

On this day, the accomplishments and achievements of women are celebrated around the world. Barriers to women achieving their God-given purpose and mandates are also highlighted. It is important to know that all human beings, including women, were created for a purpose and to fulfill a mandate on the earth.

It does not matter what corner of the earth you find yourself; you can still make a difference and impact the lives of those around you. Whatever that looks like for you, whether as a daughter, friend, wife, mother, boss, inventor, teacher, or prophetess, you are making a difference! Don't let man-made barriers stop you.

Press into God and fulfill your true purpose in Him. In your pursuit of purpose, remember that the most important thing is a woman who fears the Lord, and she shall be greatly praised.

Reflect
In what ways have you made a difference as a woman? What can you do to continue to make an impact in your world? What are the barriers to making a difference?

Pray
Heavenly Father, thank You for creating women. Thank You for the impact of women in our generation and beyond. Give us the wisdom to remove every barrier preventing women from becoming all You created them to be. Help us support women to achieve their God-given potential. In Jesus' name I pray. Amen.

Practical Applications
1. Wish yourself (if you are a woman) or the women in your life a Happy International Women's Day.
2. Celebrate your accomplishments, no matter how seemingly insignificant.
3. Support the goals of the women in your life.

— • —

ABOUT THE AUTHOR

Dr. Obot Tigah, DNP, WHNP-BC, is the founder of Girls with Standards and a strategic coach at the Girls with Standards Academy. Dr. Obot is a woman of the word and prayer, and she is passionate about helping women live out their God-given purpose. She is the author of Love is Blind, Marriage is the Eye-Opener. She has a Doctor of Nursing Practice degree, with a specialization in Women's Health and Education. Dr. Obot lives in Pennsylvania, United States, with her husband and two children. In her spare time, she enjoys traveling, reading, and spending time with her family and friends.

For speaking engagements, please contact:
Dr. Obot Tigah via email – obot@girlswithstandards.com

ObotTigah | **Girls with Standards**

Order my book

Visit the website

Join a vibrant community of young/adult women

Join & Learn about GWS Academy

Join our 3 days monthly Prayer & Fasting

Check our socials

SCAN ME

Dr. Obot Tigah | Instagram, Facebook, TikTok
Daughter of God | Founder, Girls With Standards | Dr. WHAP | Author | Teacher

https://linktr.ee/Obot.Tigah

www.girlswithstandards.com

girls_withstandards

giriswithstandards

LIVE BY HIGH STANDARDS GUIDED DEVOTIONAL JOURNAL

is your space to respond, reflect, and be spiritually accountable.

Whether you pair it with the Live by High Standards devotional or use it alone, it helps you:

- Record what God is showing you
- Track how God is shifting your thoughts
- Write out your prayers and declarations
- Anchor your growth in truth, not emotion

This journal is for the woman who's not just reading the truth but responding to it.

HAVE YOU EVER WONDERED...

Why everything felt perfect until after the vows?

In a culture that glorifies chemistry and forgets covenant, *Love Is Blind, Marriage Is the Eye-Opener* is an invitation to **see clearly, before and after "I do."**

It helps you see what love alone cannot show you, and what prayer, wisdom, and the Word can.

This book is not a warning. **It is a wake-up call to not just pray for marriage, but to prepare for it.**

Made in the USA
Monee, IL
10 August 2025

22174410R00056